THE ABCs OF BMX

Riding through the Alphabet

BY MICHAEL MOSIER

DEDICATION

TO MY SON, LEVI,

IN EVERY PAGE TURNED,
AND EVERY STORY TOLD,
MAY YOU FIND THE SAME
INSPIRATION, JOY, AND WONDER
THAT YOU BRING TO MY LIFE
EACH DAY.

WITH ALL MY LOVE,
DADDY

A IS FOR AGILITY

With agility, we're swift and spry,
zipping around, touching the sky!
With every swerve and little jive,
agility keeps our racing alive!

B IS FOR BALANCE BIKE

No pedals, just wheels on our balance bike,
pushing along, feeling the hike.
It teaches us balance, it teaches us grace,
preparing us for the big BMX race!

C IS FOR CORNERING

Around each corner, smoothly we tend,
hugging the bend, making our way,
not a second to spend.

D IS FOR DRAFTING

Riding close behind with drafting's design,
using less energy, feeling so fine.
The wind can't touch us, we're in a line!

To race 'til the end, round each tricky bend,
endurance is our lasting friend.
Even when tired, we don't descend!

F IS FOR FINISH LINE

Where the crowd cheers and racers combine,
we all dream of crossing that finish line.
A moment of victory, feeling divine!

G IS FOR GEAR

Helmets, gloves, pads on the rear,
dressed up in protective BMX gear.
Safe and sound, with nothing to fear!

On our head, it snugly sits,
protecting our brains, keeping us fit.
In every race, helmets are a hit!

I IS FOR INTERVALS

We ride fast, then take it slow,
intervals help our stamina grow.
Alternating rhythms, we go with the flow!

J IS FOR JUMP

Up the ramp, into the sky,
we love to make our BMX bikes fly!
Jumps give a thrill,
making time stand still.

K IS FOR KICK

A quick boost right from the start,
a sudden kick, racing's art!
With this burst, we're sharp and smart!

L IS FOR LINE CHOICE

Picking the path, avoiding the crash,
with a good line choice,
through tracks, we dash!

M IS FOR MOMENTUM

Racing down hills, feeling the chills,
momentum propels us, it's such a thrill!

N IS FOR NUTRITION

Fruits, proteins, and a hydration solution,
give us the strength through proper nutrition.
For the race, we need the right contribution!

Sometimes we slide, just a tad to the side.
Oversteer can happen, but we ride with pride!

P IS FOR PACING

Not too quick, with a rhythm so slick,
pacing helps us cover ground brick by brick.

Q IS FOR QUICK START

When the whistle blows, away we dart!
Getting ahead is the quick start's art.

R IS FOR RIDING POSITION

Sit firm, sit tight, holding the handle, just right.
Riding position is key, making our racing light!

S IS FOR SPORTSMANSHIP

On the BMX track or off,
being kind and fair is the way to rock!
Whether you win or face a slip,
it's sportsmanship that makes you truly hip.
Celebrating others, taking defeat in stride,
with sportsmanship, every racer has pride.

Day after day, in sun or when raining
perfecting our moves is the goal of training.

U IS FOR UNDERSTEER

When turns are tight
and we have to steer clear,
sometimes we face
what they call understeer!

Speeding away, come what may,
in BMX racing, velocity's the way!

When BMX riders take a stand,
lifting the front wheel off the land,
with balance and a special skill,
they ride on one wheel for a thrilling thrill!

A grand stage where champions claim,
showcasing their skills, it's the X Games' fame!

Y IS FOR YELL

Cheering on mates, as they accelerate,
with every yell, our spirits elevate.
It's the sound of the crowd, vibrant and loud,
making each racer stand tall and proud.

Fast as lightning, it's so exciting!
Racing away, we zoom all day!

Made in the USA
Las Vegas, NV
10 March 2026

43333430R00019